ASOGWA JOY LOVE

Pathways to Triumph

Contents

1

The First Step

Eli Parker sat in the dusty attic of his late grandfather's house, surrounded by stacks of old books and forgotten relics. The air was thick with the smell of aged paper and memories. He wiped a bead of sweat from his brow, his fingers tracing the intricate patterns on a small, wooden box he'd found hidden under a loose floorboard. Inside, among the clutter of yellowed letters and tarnished trinkets, lay an ancient-looking book with a leather cover.

He picked it up, the leather cool and supple under his touch. It felt significant, as though it had a weight beyond its physical presence. There was no title, no author's name, just a blank cover that seemed to absorb the dim light filtering through the attic window. Eli's heart raced with a mixture of excitement and curiosity as he carefully opened the book.

The pages were blank.

Confused, Eli flipped through the book, page after page of pristine, empty parchment. Disappointment began to settle in his chest. He had hoped for some forgotten wisdom, a secret passed down through generations, but it seemed he had found nothing more than an old notebook. Frustrated, he tossed the book onto a nearby pile and turned back to the box, searching for anything else of interest.

As he rifled through the box, something caught his eye. A small, folded piece of paper tucked into the lining of the box. He pulled it out and unfolded it, revealing a short note written in a spidery, elegant script.

"To find the path to triumph, you must first face the trials. Seek the words in moments of challenge. — H.P."

Eli's mind raced. H.P. His grandfather, Henry Parker. Could this be a clue? He picked up the book again, his fingers trembling slightly. If the note was to be believed, the book wasn't blank—it was waiting for something. A trigger, perhaps.

Determined to uncover the mystery, Eli decided to start with the letters in the box. He sifted through them, each one a piece of his grandfather's life, filled with anecdotes and musings. One letter, in particular, caught his attention. It was addressed to a close friend of his grandfather, a man named Samuel. The letter detailed an adventurous journey and mentioned a cryptic message that Henry had found during his travels.

Eli's eyes widened as he read the letter. The message was hidden within the lines of a poem, a puzzle that his grandfather had spent years trying to decode. Eli scanned the poem, his mind racing as he tried to make sense of the words.

"*In shadows cast and light unseen, a journey marked by what has been. The first of steps, a truth revealed, in hearts of stone and wounds unhealed.*"

The words seemed to pulse with energy, each line a riddle begging to be solved. Eli grabbed a notebook and began to jot down notes, connecting dots and forming theories. Hours passed as he immersed himself in the puzzle, the world outside the attic forgotten.

As evening fell, Eli's eyes began to blur with exhaustion. He rubbed his temples, frustration gnawing at him. The poem was like a maze with no clear exit. He decided to take a break, stepping outside to breathe in the cool night air.

The sky was a deep indigo, stars glittering like diamonds scattered across a velvet blanket. Eli took a deep breath, letting the quiet calm his mind. He closed his eyes, the lines of the poem running through his thoughts. "*In shadows cast and light unseen...*"

A sudden realization struck him. Shadows and light. The attic had been dim, but what if he needed more light to see what was hidden? He rushed back inside, his heart pounding.

Back in the attic, Eli retrieved the book and positioned it under the brightest lamp he could find. He opened it to the first page and held his breath. Slowly, almost imperceptibly, words began to appear on the blank page, as if written by an invisible hand.

"*To begin the journey, seek the key in the place where shadows and light meet.*"

Eli's pulse quickened. The message was clear, but its meaning was still shrouded in mystery. He scanned the attic, looking for a clue. His gaze fell on the old mirror in the corner, half-covered with a dusty sheet. Mirrors reflected light and cast shadows. Could this be it?

He approached the mirror, his reflection staring back at him, eyes wide with anticipation. He touched the frame, feeling for anything unusual. His fingers brushed against a small latch on the side. With a soft click, the back of the mirror opened to reveal a hidden compartment.

Inside was a small, ornate key.

Eli's heart raced as he took the key in his hand. This was the first step, the beginning of a journey that promised to be unlike anything he had ever imagined. The path to triumph lay before him, hidden in shadows and light, waiting to be discovered.

As he held the key, the words in the book faded away, leaving the page blank once more. But Eli knew he had unlocked something far greater than an old family secret. He had unlocked the first chapter of his own destiny.

2

Hidden Trials

Eli's heart pounded as he held the small, ornate key. The weight of it felt substantial, its cool metal pressing against his palm. He knew this key was a crucial piece of the puzzle, but to what lock did it belong? His grandfather's cryptic note echoed in his mind: "Seek the words in moments of challenge."

He descended the narrow attic stairs, each creak of the wooden steps amplifying the silence of the old house. Eli's eyes scanned the rooms as he moved, searching for anything that might give him a clue. The key seemed too significant to be meant for something ordinary.

In the study, he found more letters and documents piled neatly on the oak desk. Eli sifted through them, his eyes darting over the faded ink. Among the mundane correspondence, he found another letter addressed to Samuel. This one was dated years after the first, and Eli read it with mounting excitement.

"Samuel, I believe I've found the first key, but the true test lies ahead. The answer is hidden where shadows play, and only the worthy will find their way. — H.P."

Eli's gaze shifted to the dark corners of the study. The late afternoon sun cast long shadows across the room, stretching and twisting with the setting sun. He thought about his grandfather's words. Where shadows play. The phrase seemed familiar, yet elusive.

A sudden gust of wind rattled the window, startling Eli. He moved to close it and noticed an old painting on the wall, partially obscured by shadow. It depicted a lush garden with winding paths and hidden alcoves. Eli's fingers traced the frame, his breath catching as he noticed a small indentation—a keyhole.

With a mixture of apprehension and excitement, Eli inserted the key into the lock. It fit perfectly. He turned it slowly, the mechanisms within the frame clicking into place. The painting swung open like a door, revealing a hidden compartment. Inside, there was another piece of parchment.

Eli unfolded the parchment, revealing another poem:

"*Beyond the garden's secret gate, the trials of the worthy await. Through fire and stone, the path will wind, seek the light, and the truth you'll find.*"

The garden. Eli's mind raced back to the letter and the painting. He needed to find this garden, but where could it be? He remembered a photograph he had seen earlier, tucked in one of the books on the desk. It showed his grandfather standing beside a wrought iron gate, vines curling around its edges. The same gate from the painting.

Determined, Eli grabbed his coat and made his way outside. The sun was dipping below the horizon, casting the world in a dusky glow. He followed the path around the house, his steps quickening as he neared the back. There, half-hidden by overgrown bushes, was the gate from the photograph.

He pushed it open, the hinges groaning in protest. The garden beyond was wild and untamed, nature reclaiming what had once been meticulously maintained. Eli felt a shiver of anticipation as he stepped inside. The air was cooler here, the shadows deeper. He knew he was on the right track.

Eli navigated through the garden, following the winding paths described in the poem. Each step seemed to take him deeper into the past, the memories of his grandfather's voice whispering in the rustle of leaves. The garden seemed to pulse with life, the air thick with the scent of earth and blooming flowers.

He reached a clearing where an ancient stone archway stood, its surface weathered by time. The archway led to a dark tunnel, the entrance partially obscured by creeping ivy. Eli hesitated for a moment, the fear of the unknown gripping him. But he knew he had to press on. This was the trial, the challenge he had to face.

With a deep breath, he stepped through the archway. The tunnel was dark and cool, the walls damp and slick. His footsteps echoed in the confined space, each sound amplifying his sense of isolation. The darkness seemed to close in around him, but Eli pressed forward, his mind fixed on the promise of light at the end.

Suddenly, the tunnel opened into a cavernous room. Torches lined the walls, casting flickering light over ancient stone carvings. In the center of the room was a pedestal, and atop it sat a small, intricately carved box. Eli approached it cautiously, his pulse quickening.

As he reached out to touch the box, a deep rumble shook the ground. The carvings on the walls seemed to come alive, shadows dancing in the torchlight. Eli stepped back, heart pounding. The trial had begun.

He glanced around, searching for clues. The carvings depicted scenes of fire and stone, paths winding through perilous landscapes. Eli realized he had to decipher the meaning of these images to proceed. His eyes landed on a particular carving—a man holding a torch, lighting his way through darkness.

Eli grabbed a nearby torch and held it up, casting light on the carvings. The shadows shifted, revealing hidden symbols and paths. He traced the patterns with his fingers, piecing together the story they told. The man in the carving had found his way by following the light, even when the path was treacherous.

Taking a deep breath, Eli mimicked the actions of the man in the carving. He moved through the cavern, using the torch to reveal hidden pathways. Each step was a leap of faith, the ground seeming to shift beneath him. But he pressed on, his determination unwavering.

Finally, he reached a small alcove where another key rested on a stone pedestal. He took it, feeling a sense of accomplishment wash over him. The key was warm in his hand, as though it held a piece of the journey within it.

As Eli exited the cavern, the words of the poem echoed in his mind. "*Seek the light, and the truth you'll find.*" He knew this was just the beginning of his trials, but he felt ready. He had faced the darkness and found his way through. The path to triumph was long and uncertain, but Eli was determined to see it through to the end.

3

The Mentor's Legacy

The cavern's exit led Eli back into the garden, where the twilight had given way to night. The moon cast a silvery glow over the landscape, making the garden seem almost otherworldly. Eli clutched the warm key in his hand, its intricate design shimmering faintly in the moonlight. He felt a strange mix of exhilaration and trepidation; he had overcome the first trial, but he knew more challenges awaited.

Eli made his way back to the house, his thoughts racing. The poem had mentioned the "trials of the worthy," and he couldn't shake the feeling that the next clue was hidden somewhere within his grandfather's belongings. He climbed the stairs to the study, the shadows cast by the flickering candlelight dancing on the walls. The key felt heavier in his pocket as he approached his grandfather's old desk.

He rummaged through the drawers, searching for anything that might reveal the next step. His fingers brushed against a leather-bound journal tucked away in the back of a drawer. Eli pulled it out and opened it, the pages filled with his grandfather's neat handwriting. The journal chronicled his grandfather's adventures, but one entry stood out.

"*June 14, 1982. Today, I met with Samuel. He shared with me a secret he discovered during his time in the East. It's a key to understanding the trials, a way to unlock the hidden wisdom within the book. I must be cautious, for there are those who would seek to use this knowledge for their own gain.*"

Eli's heart raced as he read the entry. Samuel again. His grandfather's trusted friend seemed to hold many of the answers. Eli remembered an old photograph of Samuel and his grandfather taken at a cabin in the mountains. The cabin had been their retreat, a place of quiet reflection and learning. Eli realized he needed to visit that cabin.

The next morning, Eli set off for the mountains, the journal and the key safely tucked in his bag. The drive was long, the winding roads leading him higher into the wilderness. The cabin, nestled among tall pine trees, looked almost exactly as it did in the photograph. Eli felt a sense of reverence as he approached, knowing that his grandfather and Samuel had spent countless hours here, unraveling the mysteries of the world.

The cabin's door creaked open, revealing a cozy interior. Eli explored the rooms, looking for anything that might guide him. In the living room, he found a large, dusty bookshelf filled with ancient tomes and manuscripts. One book in particular caught his eye—a thick, leather-bound volume titled "The Trials of the Worthy."

Eli pulled the book from the shelf and opened it. The pages were filled with detailed illustrations and descriptions of various trials, each designed to test the resolve and wisdom of the seeker. One section, marked with a ribbon, detailed a trial called "The Whispering Winds." The trial involved deciphering a series of coded messages hidden within the sounds of the wind.

Eli stepped outside, the cool mountain air filling his lungs. The wind rustled through the trees, creating a symphony of whispers. He closed his eyes, focusing on the sounds. At first, it seemed like mere noise, but gradually, he began to discern patterns within the whispers—snatches of words and phrases that seemed to form a coherent message.

"*In the place where the eagle soars, the first message awaits. Seek the stone of wisdom, and the path will be made clear.*"

Eli's eyes snapped open. The place where the eagle soars. He recalled a rocky outcrop near the cabin, a place where eagles were known to nest. He made his way there, the whispers of the wind guiding him. The outcrop offered a breathtaking view of the valley below, the mountains stretching out in all directions.

As he scanned the area, his eyes fell upon a large stone partially hidden among the rocks. The stone was engraved with intricate symbols, similar to those he had seen in the cavern. Eli knelt beside it, running his fingers over the carvings. The symbols seemed to pulse with energy, guiding him to a small, hidden compartment within the stone.

Inside the compartment was another key, this one made of silver and shaped like an eagle in flight. Eli's heart pounded as he took the key, knowing it was another piece of the puzzle. But there was something else in the compartment—a rolled-up piece of parchment. Eli carefully unrolled it, revealing a map of the mountains with several locations marked.

Each marked location was accompanied by a symbol, each representing a different trial. Eli knew this map would guide him through the next stages of his journey. But he also knew he couldn't do it alone. He needed help— someone who understood the trials as deeply as his grandfather and Samuel did.

Eli's thoughts turned to an old family friend, Dr. Alice Bennett, a renowned historian and expert in ancient mysteries. She had been a close confidante of his grandfather and had often spoken of the trials in hushed tones. Eli decided to visit her, hoping she could shed light on the path ahead.

The drive to Dr. Bennett's house was filled with anticipation. Eli's mind raced with questions. What would she know about the trials? Could she help him decipher the map? When he arrived, Dr. Bennett greeted him warmly, her eyes twinkling with curiosity as Eli explained his discoveries.

She listened intently, nodding as he recounted his journey. "Your grandfather was a remarkable man," she said, her voice filled with admiration. "He and Samuel uncovered many secrets, but they always knew the trials were meant to be faced by those who were truly worthy. I will help you, Eli, but you must be prepared for the challenges ahead. The trials will test you in ways you cannot imagine."

Eli nodded, determination burning in his eyes. He had come too far to turn back now. With Dr. Bennett's guidance, he felt ready to face whatever lay ahead. The path to triumph was fraught with peril, but Eli was resolved to see it through. The legacy of his grandfather and the secrets of the trials were within his grasp, and he would not rest until he had uncovered the truth.

As they pored over the map together, Eli felt a renewed sense of purpose. The next trial awaited, and with each step, he drew closer to unlocking the wisdom hidden within the book. The journey was far from over, but Eli knew he was on the right path, guided by the legacy of those who had come before him.

4

Whispers in the Dark

The wind howled outside Dr. Bennett's study, rattling the windows and sending chills down Eli's spine. He and Dr. Bennett huddled over the map, the soft glow of a lamp casting long shadows on the walls. The map marked several locations, each one accompanied by an enigmatic symbol representing different trials. They had decided to start with the nearest location, an ancient forest known as Whispering Woods.

"Are you sure about this?" Dr. Bennett asked, her brow furrowed with concern.

Eli nodded resolutely. "I have to be. I need to understand my grandfather's legacy, and this is the only way."

Dr. Bennett sighed but nodded. "Very well. Whispering Woods is known for its treacherous paths and eerie sounds. Be prepared for anything."

Eli packed a small bag with essentials and set off early the next morning. The forest loomed in the distance, a dark mass against the rising sun. As he approached, the trees seemed to swallow the light, creating a foreboding canopy overhead. The air grew cooler, the silence broken only by the occasional rustle of leaves and distant bird calls.

He entered the forest, the dense foliage closing around him. The path was narrow and winding, the ground uneven beneath his feet. Every step felt like a descent into another world, a place where time seemed to stand still. The deeper he went, the more oppressive the atmosphere became. Shadows flitted between the trees, and Eli couldn't shake the feeling that he was being watched.

He stopped to catch his breath, the silence pressing in on him. That's when he heard it—a faint whisper, barely audible over the rustling leaves. Eli strained to listen, but the whispering stopped as suddenly as it had begun. He shook his head, chalking it up to his imagination, and pressed on.

The path led to a clearing where an ancient stone altar stood, covered in moss and ivy. Eli approached it cautiously, his eyes scanning the surroundings for any sign of danger. The altar was inscribed with runes similar to those he had seen in the cavern and on the stone in the mountains. He brushed away the moss, revealing a faintly glowing symbol—a crescent moon.

Eli pulled out the map, noting that the crescent moon symbol matched the one marked at this location. He felt a surge of excitement; he was on the right track. As he examined the altar, the whispering started again, louder this time. The words were still indistinct, but they seemed to be coming from all around him.

"Who's there?" Eli called out, his voice trembling slightly. There was no response, only the continuous whispering that seemed to grow more insistent.

Eli's heart pounded in his chest. He had faced darkness and trials before, but this felt different—more personal, more menacing. He took a deep breath, trying to steady his nerves. "Focus," he told himself. "Remember the poem."

He recited the poem from the journal in his mind: "*In the place where shadows play, listen close to what they say.*" The whispers must be a clue, he realized. He closed his eyes, trying to focus on the sound. The whispers seemed to form patterns, fragments of words that began to make sense.

"*Seek... the... heart... of... the... forest...*"

Eli's eyes snapped open. The heart of the forest. He scanned the clearing, searching for any indication of where to go next. His eyes landed on a narrow path leading deeper into the woods. The path was overgrown, barely visible, but it seemed to call to him.

He followed the path, the whispering guiding him. The forest grew denser, the trees taller and more imposing. The air was thick with anticipation, each step bringing him closer to the unknown. The whispering grew louder, more coherent, guiding him like an invisible hand.

Finally, he emerged into another clearing, this one dominated by an enormous tree with gnarled roots and thick branches that seemed to touch the sky. The tree's bark was covered in more runes, and at its base was a small, ancient-looking chest.

Eli approached the chest cautiously. The whispers were almost deafening now, urging him forward. He knelt beside the chest, his fingers trembling as he lifted the lid. Inside was a single item—a small, intricately carved pendant in the shape of a crescent moon. He picked it up, feeling a strange energy emanating from it.

As he held the pendant, the whispering stopped abruptly, leaving an eerie silence in its wake. Eli's pulse quickened. He knew this pendant was important, but its purpose was still unclear. He slipped it into his pocket and turned to leave, but the path he had taken was no longer there. The forest seemed to shift around him, the trees closing in and cutting off his escape.

Panic surged through him. He was trapped. He spun around, searching for another way out, but the forest seemed impenetrable. The whispering returned, softer this time, almost soothing. It guided him to the tree once more. Eli realized he had missed something. He examined the runes more closely, noting that they seemed to form a pattern.

"*Courage in the face of darkness, wisdom in the heart of the storm,*" Eli muttered, piecing together the meaning. The pendant was the key, but to what?

He noticed a small indentation in the tree's trunk, shaped like the pendant. With a deep breath, he inserted the pendant into the indentation. The tree shuddered, and a hidden door swung open, revealing a narrow staircase descending into darkness.

Eli hesitated only for a moment before stepping inside. The staircase spiraled downward, the air growing colder with each step. The whispers had faded, replaced by a deep, almost tangible silence. He reached the bottom of the stairs and found himself in a cavernous chamber, lit by a soft, otherworldly glow.

In the center of the chamber was a pedestal, and atop it, a large, ancient book. Eli approached it cautiously, his heart pounding in his chest. The book's cover was inscribed with the same runes he had seen before, and as he opened it, the pages began to fill with words.

"*To the seeker who has faced the trials and listened to the whispers, you have proven your worth. The path to triumph lies within these pages, but beware, for the journey is far from over.*"

Eli felt a surge of determination. He had come this far and uncovered so much, but he knew the real challenges were just beginning. With the book in hand, he made his way back up the stairs, ready to face whatever trials lay ahead.

The path to triumph was long and fraught with danger, but Eli was resolved to see it through to the end, guided by the whispers in the dark and the legacy of those who had come before him.

5

The Labyrinth of Lost Souls

The morning sun cast long shadows as Eli ventured toward the next location marked on his map: the Labyrinth of Lost Souls. The ancient book described the labyrinth as a place where many had entered but few had emerged, their souls forever wandering its dark corridors. Eli felt a knot of anxiety tighten in his stomach, but he knew he had to press on. Each trial brought him closer to unlocking the secrets of his grandfather's legacy.

The labyrinth was hidden deep within an old forest, the entrance obscured by overgrown vegetation and ancient stone pillars. The air was thick with the scent of damp earth and decaying leaves, the only sounds the distant cawing of crows and the occasional rustle of leaves. Eli stood before the entrance, a gaping maw of darkness that seemed to beckon him forward.

He took a deep breath and stepped inside, the shadows swallowing him whole. The temperature dropped sharply, the air growing colder and more oppressive. Eli switched on his flashlight, the beam cutting through the darkness and illuminating the narrow passage ahead. The walls were lined with carvings and symbols, their meanings lost to time.

Eli pressed on, the path twisting and turning in disorienting ways. The silence was almost deafening, broken only by the sound of his own footsteps echoing off the stone walls. He felt a growing sense of unease, as if unseen eyes were watching his every move.

At a fork in the path, Eli paused, consulting the book. The pages had shown no clear map of the labyrinth, only vague hints and cryptic passages. One line stood out to him: "*Trust not the eyes but the heart; the light will guide you in the dark.*"

He closed his eyes, taking a moment to steady his breathing. The pendant he had found at Whispering Woods hung around his neck, its crescent shape warm against his skin. He reached out with his senses, feeling for any hint of a guiding presence. A faint tug seemed to pull him to the right, and he followed it, hoping his instincts were leading him true.

The passage widened into a large chamber, the ceiling lost in shadows. At the center stood a stone altar, much like the one he had encountered before. Surrounding the altar were statues of hooded figures, their faces obscured and their hands outstretched as if in supplication.

Eli approached the altar, the pendant growing warmer against his chest. He placed his hands on the cold stone, feeling a faint vibration beneath his fingers. The whispers began again, soft and indistinct, filling the chamber with an eerie chorus.

"*Seek the light within the shadows,*" the whispers seemed to say.

Eli glanced around, his flashlight revealing nothing but stone and darkness. He turned off the beam, plunging the chamber into pitch blackness. For a moment, there was only silence and the sound of his own heartbeat.

Then, faintly at first, he saw a glow emanating from one of the statues. Eli approached it, the glow growing brighter as he drew near. The statue's hands were cupped around a small, glowing orb, its light pulsating gently. Eli reached out, and the orb's light flared, illuminating a hidden passage at the back of the chamber.

He entered the passage, the orb's light guiding his way. The walls were narrower here, the air colder. The whispers grew louder, more insistent, as if urging him onward. The passage twisted and turned, leading him deeper into the labyrinth.

Eli emerged into another chamber, this one filled with mirrors of all shapes and sizes. The reflections seemed to move on their own, distorting and shifting in the dim light. Eli felt a sense of disorientation, as if the mirrors were playing tricks on his mind.

He took a step forward, and the mirrors seemed to close in around him, their surfaces shimmering with an unnatural light. Eli's reflection stared back at him from every angle, each one slightly different, slightly distorted. The whispers grew louder, more chaotic, filling the chamber with a cacophony of sound.

"*Face the truth within,*" the whispers seemed to chant.

Eli steeled himself, focusing on the reflections. He saw himself as a child, as a teenager, as an adult, each stage of his life reflected back at him in vivid detail. The mirrors showed his fears, his regrets, his triumphs, and his failures. They showed his insecurities and doubts, the moments of weakness and strength that had shaped him.

Eli felt a surge of emotion, the reflections overwhelming him with their intensity. He closed his eyes, taking a deep breath. The poem from the book echoed in his mind: "*Courage in the face of darkness, wisdom in the heart of the storm.*"

He opened his eyes, meeting his own gaze in the nearest mirror. "I am not defined by my past," he said aloud, his voice steady. "I am not my fears or my failures. I am more than my reflection."

The mirrors seemed to shimmer and shift, the reflections growing clearer and more focused. The whispers softened, becoming a gentle murmur. Eli stepped forward, reaching out to touch the nearest mirror. The surface rippled like water, and his hand passed through, revealing a hidden compartment behind it.

Inside the compartment was another artifact, a small, intricately carved key. Eli took it, feeling a sense of accomplishment. He had faced his own reflections and emerged stronger. The whispers faded, leaving a profound silence in their wake.

Eli turned to leave, the path back to the entrance illuminated by the orb's light. As he exited the labyrinth, he felt a renewed sense of purpose. Each trial was teaching him more about himself and the legacy he sought to understand. The key in his hand was another piece of the puzzle, another step on the path to triumph.

The journey was far from over, but Eli felt ready for whatever lay ahead. With the book, the pendant, and the key as his guides, he set off for the next location on the map, determined to uncover the truth and honor the legacy of his grandfather. The labyrinth had tested him, but he had emerged stronger, more resolute in his quest for knowledge and understanding.

6

The Labyrinth of Lost Souls

The morning sun cast long shadows as Eli ventured toward the next location marked on his map: the Labyrinth of Lost Souls. The ancient book described the labyrinth as a place where many had entered but few had emerged, their souls forever wandering its dark corridors. Eli felt a knot of anxiety tighten in his stomach, but he knew he had to press on. Each trial brought him closer to unlocking the secrets of his grandfather's legacy.

The labyrinth was hidden deep within an old forest, the entrance obscured by overgrown vegetation and ancient stone pillars. The air was thick with the scent of damp earth and decaying leaves, the only sounds the distant cawing of crows and the occasional rustle of leaves. Eli stood before the entrance, a gaping maw of darkness that seemed to beckon him forward.

He took a deep breath and stepped inside, the shadows swallowing him whole. The temperature dropped sharply, the air growing colder and more oppressive. Eli switched on his flashlight, the beam cutting through the darkness and illuminating the narrow passage ahead. The walls were lined with carvings and symbols, their meanings lost to time.

Eli pressed on, the path twisting and turning in disorienting ways. The silence was almost deafening, broken only by the sound of his own footsteps echoing off the stone walls. He felt a growing sense of unease, as if unseen eyes were watching his every move.

At a fork in the path, Eli paused, consulting the book. The pages had shown no clear map of the labyrinth, only vague hints and cryptic passages. One line stood out to him: "*Trust not the eyes but the heart; the light will guide you in the dark.*"

He closed his eyes, taking a moment to steady his breathing. The pendant he had found at Whispering Woods hung around his neck, its crescent shape warm against his skin. He reached out with his senses, feeling for any hint of a guiding presence. A faint tug seemed to pull him to the right, and he followed it, hoping his instincts were leading him true.

The passage widened into a large chamber, the ceiling lost in shadows. At the center stood a stone altar, much like the one he had encountered before. Surrounding the altar were statues of hooded figures, their faces obscured and their hands outstretched as if in supplication.

Eli approached the altar, the pendant growing warmer against his chest. He placed his hands on the cold stone, feeling a faint vibration beneath his fingers. The whispers began again, soft and indistinct, filling the chamber with an eerie chorus.

"*Seek the light within the shadows,*" the whispers seemed to say.

Eli glanced around, his flashlight revealing nothing but stone and darkness. He turned off the beam, plunging the chamber into pitch blackness. For a moment, there was only silence and the sound of his own heartbeat.

Then, faintly at first, he saw a glow emanating from one of the statues. Eli approached it, the glow growing brighter as he drew near. The statue's hands were cupped around a small, glowing orb, its light pulsating gently. Eli reached out, and the orb's light flared, illuminating a hidden passage at the back of the chamber.

He entered the passage, the orb's light guiding his way. The walls were narrower here, the air colder. The whispers grew louder, more insistent, as if urging him onward. The passage twisted and turned, leading him deeper into the labyrinth.

Eli emerged into another chamber, this one filled with mirrors of all shapes and sizes. The reflections seemed to move on their own, distorting and shifting in the dim light. Eli felt a sense of disorientation, as if the mirrors were playing tricks on his mind.

He took a step forward, and the mirrors seemed to close in around him, their surfaces shimmering with an unnatural light. Eli's reflection stared back at him from every angle, each one slightly different, slightly distorted. The whispers grew louder, more chaotic, filling the chamber with a cacophony of sound.

"*Face the truth within,*" the whispers seemed to chant.

Eli steeled himself, focusing on the reflections. He saw himself as a child, as a teenager, as an adult, each stage of his life reflected back at him in vivid detail. The mirrors showed his fears, his regrets, his triumphs, and his failures. They showed his insecurities and doubts, the moments of weakness and strength that had shaped him.

Eli felt a surge of emotion, the reflections overwhelming him with their intensity. He closed his eyes, taking a deep breath. The poem from the book echoed in his mind: "*Courage in the face of darkness, wisdom in the heart of the storm.*"

He opened his eyes, meeting his own gaze in the nearest mirror. "I am not defined by my past," he said aloud, his voice steady. "I am not my fears or my failures. I am more than my reflection."

The mirrors seemed to shimmer and shift, the reflections growing clearer and more focused. The whispers softened, becoming a gentle murmur. Eli stepped forward, reaching out to touch the nearest mirror. The surface rippled like water, and his hand passed through, revealing a hidden compartment behind it.

Inside the compartment was another artifact, a small, intricately carved key. Eli took it, feeling a sense of accomplishment. He had faced his own reflections and emerged stronger. The whispers faded, leaving a profound silence in their wake.

Eli turned to leave, the path back to the entrance illuminated by the orb's light. As he exited the labyrinth, he felt a renewed sense of purpose. Each trial was teaching him more about himself and the legacy he sought to understand. The key in his hand was another piece of the puzzle, another step on the path to triumph.

The journey was far from over, but Eli felt ready for whatever lay ahead. With the book, the pendant, and the key as his guides, he set off for the next location on the map, determined to uncover the truth and honor the legacy of his grandfather. The labyrinth had tested him, but he had emerged stronger, more resolute in his quest for knowledge and understanding.

7

Shadows of the Past

Eli stood at the edge of the desolate village, its buildings crumbling under the weight of time and neglect. The air was thick with the scent of decay, and an eerie silence hung over the place like a shroud. This was the place marked on his map as the next trial site—the village where his grandfather had spent his final days. The book mentioned it as a place where past and present intertwined, a place of forgotten memories and lingering spirits.

Eli's footsteps echoed on the cracked cobblestone streets as he made his way deeper into the village. The houses were dark and empty, their windows like hollow eyes staring out at him. He felt a chill run down his spine, but he pushed forward, driven by the need to uncover the truth.

He reached the village square, where a large, weathered statue stood. The statue depicted a hooded figure, its face obscured by shadows, holding a lantern aloft. Eli approached it, noticing an inscription at the base: "*In the darkness, the light reveals the truth.*"

Eli glanced around, spotting an old lantern hanging from a nearby post. He retrieved it, its glass cracked but intact. He fumbled for his lighter, igniting the wick and casting a flickering light across the square. The shadows danced and shifted, creating an almost hypnotic effect.

He noticed a faint trail of footprints leading away from the square, barely visible in the lantern's light. Eli followed them, the path winding through the village and into the forest beyond. The trees closed in around him, their branches forming a twisted canopy overhead. The light from the lantern cast long shadows on the ground, and Eli felt the weight of unseen eyes watching his every move.

The path led to a small, decrepit house on the outskirts of the forest. Its windows were boarded up, and the door hung loosely on its hinges. Eli felt a sense of foreboding as he approached, but he knew he had to go inside. He pushed the door open, the wood creaking ominously, and stepped into the darkness.

The air inside was musty and stale, the faint smell of rot permeating the room. Eli raised the lantern, its light revealing a room cluttered with old furniture and broken artifacts. A large, ornate mirror stood against one wall, its surface covered in a thick layer of dust.

Eli approached the mirror, wiping away the dust to reveal his reflection. For a moment, he saw only himself, but then the image began to shift and change. The room around him transformed, becoming brighter and more vibrant. He saw his grandfather, younger and full of life, working at a desk covered in papers and books.

The image shifted again, showing his grandfather speaking to a group of people. Eli recognized some of the faces from old photographs—colleagues, friends, and family members. The scene changed once more, showing his grandfather alone, writing in a journal by the light of a single candle. Eli strained to see the words, but they were blurred and indistinct.

Suddenly, the room grew cold, and the image in the mirror darkened. Eli saw shadows creeping into the room, surrounding his grandfather. The figure at the desk looked up, fear etched on his face. The shadows closed in, and the image faded to black.

Eli stepped back, his heart racing. He knew he had to find that journal. It held the key to understanding his grandfather's final days. He searched the room, his hands trembling as he sifted through the debris. Finally, in a drawer beneath the desk, he found it—an old, leather-bound journal, its pages yellowed with age.

He opened the journal, the lantern's light illuminating the delicate script. The entries detailed his grandfather's research, his discoveries, and his growing fear of the shadows that seemed to haunt him. Eli read on, the words painting a picture of a man driven by a desperate need to uncover the truth, yet tormented by the darkness that pursued him.

The final entry was dated the day before his grandfather's disappearance. It spoke of a hidden chamber beneath the village, a place where the past and present converged. Eli felt a surge of determination. He had to find that chamber.

He left the house, the journal clutched tightly in his hand, and made his way back to the village. The lantern flickered as he navigated the narrow streets, the shadows seeming to follow him. He reached the village square and examined the statue once more. The lantern in the statue's hand glowed faintly, its light pointing toward a small, unmarked building at the edge of the square.

Eli approached the building, feeling a sense of anticipation. The door was locked, but the key he had found in the labyrinth fit perfectly. He turned the key, and the door swung open with a creak.

Inside, a narrow staircase led down into the darkness. Eli took a deep breath and descended, the air growing colder with each step. The lantern's light cast eerie shadows on the walls, and Eli felt the weight of history pressing down on him.

The staircase ended in a large, underground chamber. The walls were lined with shelves filled with books and artifacts, and in the center of the room stood a large stone altar. Eli approached the altar, noticing a series of runes carved into its surface. He placed the journal on the altar, and the runes began to glow with a soft, blue light.

The shadows in the chamber shifted, coalescing into the form of his grandfather. The figure looked at Eli, a mixture of sadness and relief in his eyes. "You've come," the figure said, his voice echoing in the chamber.

Eli felt a lump in his throat. "Grandfather? What happened to you?"

The figure sighed. "The darkness... it consumed me. I was so close to uncovering the truth, but I was too late. The shadows took me, trapping my soul here. But you... you can finish what I started."

Eli felt a surge of determination. "Tell me what I need to do."

The figure pointed to the journal. "The answers are within. You must complete the ritual, unlock the final secret. Only then will the shadows be dispelled, and my soul set free."

Eli nodded, opening the journal to the final pages. The instructions were clear, detailing a ritual that required the artifacts he had collected. He placed the pendant, the key, and the sphere on the altar, following the steps outlined in the journal.

As he completed the ritual, the runes on the altar glowed brighter, and the shadows in the chamber began to recede. The figure of his grandfather smiled, his form growing fainter. "Thank you, Eli. You have done what I could not. The legacy is yours to continue."

With those words, the figure faded away, and the chamber was filled with a warm, golden light. Eli felt a sense of peace wash over him. He had faced the shadows of the past and emerged stronger.

As he left the chamber, the village seemed brighter, the oppressive darkness lifted. Eli knew there were more trials ahead, but he felt ready. With the knowledge he had gained and the legacy of his grandfather guiding him, he was prepared to face whatever challenges lay ahead on the path to triumph.

8

The Phantom of Forsaken Manor

Eli stood before the iron gates of Forsaken Manor, the next location marked on his map. The manor loomed ominously in the twilight, its once-grand facade now marred by years of neglect and decay. Vines crept up the walls, and shattered windows gaped like empty eyes. The air was thick with an unnatural chill, and the rustling leaves whispered secrets of the past.

Taking a deep breath, Eli pushed open the gates. They groaned in protest, the sound echoing through the deserted grounds. He walked up the overgrown path, his steps crunching on the gravel. As he reached the front door, it swung open on its own, as if inviting him inside. The darkness beyond the threshold seemed almost alive, pulsing with unseen energy.

Eli stepped inside, his flashlight piercing the gloom. The interior of the manor was a stark contrast to its dilapidated exterior. Dust-covered chandeliers hung from the ceiling, and faded tapestries adorned the walls. The air was thick with the scent of mildew and age. He could almost hear the echoes of laughter and conversation from long ago.

He moved cautiously through the entrance hall, his footsteps muffled by the thick carpet. The book had mentioned Forsaken Manor as a place of great importance to his grandfather's research—a place where secrets were buried and the line between the living and the dead blurred. Eli's senses were on high alert, every creak and groan of the old house sending a shiver down his spine.

He found a large, ornate staircase leading to the upper floors and began to ascend, each step accompanied by the eerie sound of wood protesting beneath his weight. At the top, he turned down a long corridor lined with doors. One door at the end of the hall stood out, slightly ajar, a faint light spilling out into the hallway.

Eli approached the door, his heart pounding. As he pushed it open, he found himself in a grand library. Shelves filled with ancient books stretched from floor to ceiling, and a large fireplace dominated one wall. A fire burned low in the hearth, casting flickering shadows across the room.

On a desk near the fireplace, Eli saw an open journal. He recognized his grandfather's handwriting and felt a surge of hope. He approached the desk, his eyes scanning the pages. The entries detailed his grandfather's research into the paranormal phenomena associated with the manor. He wrote of strange apparitions, unexplained noises, and a presence that seemed to watch his every move.

Suddenly, the temperature in the room dropped, and Eli felt a cold breeze brush past him. He turned, his flashlight revealing a shadowy figure standing at the edge of the room. The figure was translucent, its features blurred, but Eli could see the outline of a woman in a flowing dress.

The figure moved closer, and Eli felt a wave of fear wash over him. He stood his ground, remembering the courage he had summoned in the labyrinth. "Who are you?" he asked, his voice steady despite the fear gnawing at him.

The figure's lips moved, but no sound came out. Eli watched as she pointed to a bookshelf on the far wall. Then, as quickly as she had appeared, she vanished, leaving only a lingering chill in the air.

Eli approached the bookshelf, his hands trembling slightly. He scanned the spines of the books, looking for any clue. His eyes fell on a large, leather-bound volume that seemed out of place. He pulled it from the shelf, revealing a hidden compartment behind it. Inside, he found a small, ornate box.

He opened the box, revealing a collection of letters and photographs. The letters were written by his grandfather and addressed to someone named Isabella. Eli read through them, piecing together a story of love and loss. His grandfather had fallen in love with Isabella, the daughter of the manor's owner, but their relationship had been doomed by the house's dark history. Isabella had died under mysterious circumstances, and her spirit was said to haunt the manor.

As Eli finished reading, he felt a sudden gust of wind, and the letters were torn from his hands, scattering across the room. The fire in the hearth flared up, casting grotesque shadows on the walls. The air was filled with a low, mournful wail.

Eli turned to see the figure of Isabella standing in the center of the room, her eyes filled with sorrow. She reached out a hand, and Eli felt an overwhelming sense of empathy. He realized that she was not a malevolent spirit but a lost soul, trapped by the unresolved pain of her past.

Summoning his courage, Eli approached her. "Isabella, I'm here to help," he said softly. "I want to understand what happened and set things right."

The figure of Isabella seemed to relax, her features softening. She pointed to the fireplace, and Eli noticed a loose brick at the base. He knelt down and pried it open, revealing another hidden compartment. Inside was a small, weathered journal—Isabella's diary.

Eli opened the diary, its pages filled with her delicate handwriting. She wrote of her love for his grandfather and the happiness they had shared. But she also wrote of the darkness that had plagued the manor—a malevolent force that had taken her life and continued to haunt the place.

As Eli read the final entries, he felt a connection to Isabella's spirit. He understood her pain and the burden she had carried. He knew that to free her, he had to confront the darkness that had claimed her life.

He stood, facing the flickering shadows in the room. "I know you're here," he said, his voice strong and clear. "I know what you did to Isabella. Show yourself!"

The room grew colder, the shadows coalescing into a dark, swirling mass. Eli felt the weight of the darkness pressing down on him, but he stood his ground. He held Isabella's diary in his hand, drawing strength from her words.

The darkness lunged at him, a palpable force of malevolence. Eli closed his eyes, focusing on the light within him. He remembered the lessons from the trials—the courage he had found, the wisdom he had gained. He opened his eyes, filled with resolve.

"Be gone!" he shouted, his voice echoing through the room. "You have no power here!"

The darkness writhed and twisted, but Eli stood firm. He felt a surge of energy, a light growing within him and radiating outward. The shadows recoiled, their strength waning. With a final, desperate cry, the darkness dissipated, leaving the room in silence.

Eli collapsed to his knees, the diary still clutched in his hand. He felt a warmth spread through the room, and when he looked up, Isabella's figure stood before him, her expression one of gratitude and peace.

"Thank you," she whispered, her voice like a soft breeze. "You have set me free."

With those words, she faded away, her spirit finally at rest. Eli felt a sense of profound accomplishment and peace. He had faced the darkness and triumphed, freeing Isabella's soul and uncovering another piece of his grandfather's legacy.

As he left Forsaken Manor, the first light of dawn began to break over the horizon. Eli felt a renewed sense of purpose. The journey was far from over, but he was ready for whatever lay ahead. With the knowledge he had gained and the strength he had found, he was prepared to face the remaining trials and uncover the full truth of his grandfather's legacy.

9

The Echoes of Eldridge Tower

Eli's footsteps reverberated through the narrow alleyways of Eldridge Tower's abandoned district. The tower loomed ahead, its skeletal silhouette against the setting sun a grim reminder of the task that lay before him. This was his final destination on the map, and the book had described it as a place of great significance—a location where the line between reality and the unknown blurred, and where the ultimate challenge awaited him.

As Eli approached, he noticed the air growing colder. An unsettling breeze whispered through the shattered windows and broken doors of surrounding buildings. The once-bustling area now felt like a ghost town, every surface coated in layers of dust and grime. The tower itself, with its crumbling stone walls and darkened windows, appeared to be a relic from a forgotten era.

The entrance to the tower was a heavy, iron door adorned with intricate engravings. Eli hesitated for a moment, feeling the weight of the decision ahead. He had come this far, faced many challenges, and uncovered many truths. Yet something about the tower filled him with an inexplicable sense of dread. Taking a deep breath, he pushed the door open, the rusty hinges groaning in protest.

Inside, the tower was a labyrinth of dark, twisting corridors and staircases. Eli's flashlight cast long, flickering shadows as he made his way deeper into the structure. The air was thick with dust, and every step stirred up small clouds that danced in the beam of light. The silence was almost palpable, broken only by the distant drip of water echoing through the emptiness.

Eli reached a large, circular chamber at the heart of the tower. The walls were lined with old, tarnished mirrors, each reflecting a distorted version of the room. In the center of the chamber stood an ornate pedestal, upon which rested an ancient-looking book, its cover adorned with strange symbols. The sight of the book sent a shiver down Eli's spine; it was as if the tower itself was daring him to uncover its secrets.

He approached the pedestal and carefully lifted the book. The moment he touched it, the room seemed to shift. The mirrors around him began to shimmer, their reflections warping and twisting. Eli's surroundings seemed to dissolve, and he found himself standing in a different place—an opulent study filled with elegant furnishings and lit by the soft glow of candlelight.

He was not alone. Seated at a large mahogany desk was a man in period clothing, his face partially obscured by shadows. The man's presence was commanding, and Eli felt an unsettling familiarity, as if he had seen him before. The man looked up, his eyes meeting Eli's with an intense gaze.

"Welcome, Eli," the man said, his voice smooth but carrying an edge of something unsettling. "I've been expecting you."

Eli's heart raced. "Who are you?"

The man smiled, a hint of darkness in his expression. "I am the guardian of this place, the keeper of its secrets. You have come seeking answers, but are you prepared for what you will find?"

Before Eli could respond, the room seemed to warp again, and he was transported back to the chamber with the mirrors. The mirrors now reflected not just the room but scenes from his own past—moments of triumph and failure, joy and sorrow. Each reflection seemed to reach out, as if trying to pull him into the past.

Eli felt a surge of panic. The mirrors showed his most painful memories, his deepest fears. He saw himself failing, losing loved ones, and facing insurmountable challenges. It was as if the tower was testing his resolve, confronting him with his own history to see if he was worthy of the ultimate truth.

He forced himself to focus, recalling the lessons he had learned from his previous trials. He remembered the courage and strength he had found within himself. With a deep breath, he stepped closer to the mirrors, determined to confront his fears.

The reflections began to change, showing not just his past but possibilities for the future. He saw himself achieving his goals, making a difference, and finding fulfillment. The mirrors shifted once more, and Eli saw the man from the study standing before him.

"The mirrors reveal what you must confront within yourself," the man said. "You have faced your past and seen the possibilities of your future. But there is one final trial, one last challenge you must overcome."

The man gestured to a hidden door behind the mirrors. "Beyond that door lies the final truth. But be warned, it will test you in ways you cannot imagine."

Eli nodded, steeling himself for what lay ahead. He approached the door, its surface covered in intricate carvings. With a deep breath, he pushed it open and stepped into a narrow passage. The walls were lined with dark, shifting shadows, and the air was heavy with an oppressive weight.

At the end of the passage, Eli emerged into a vast chamber. In the center was a large, ornate clockwork mechanism, its gears and cogs turning with a rhythmic clanking sound. The chamber was filled with the soft ticking of a thousand clocks, creating a symphony of time.

A figure stood beside the mechanism, cloaked in shadow. As Eli approached, the figure turned, revealing the face of his grandfather. The sight was both shocking and reassuring. His grandfather's eyes were filled with a mixture of pride and sadness.

"You've done well, Eli," his grandfather said. "But the final truth is not about the past or the future. It is about the present—about understanding and embracing who you are."

The clockwork mechanism began to hum, its gears shifting and aligning. Eli felt a rush of emotions as he realized what it was showing him. It was not just a machine but a representation of his own journey—a path filled with twists and turns, moments of clarity and confusion.

As the mechanism completed its cycle, the room was filled with a blinding light. Eli closed his eyes, feeling a profound sense of peace wash over him. When he opened them again, the chamber had transformed. The shadows and ticking clocks were gone, replaced by a serene landscape bathed in golden light.

His grandfather stood beside him, a gentle smile on his face. "You have completed the trials and discovered the truth within yourself. The journey was not just about uncovering the past but about understanding your own path and purpose."

Eli felt a sense of fulfillment and clarity. He had faced his fears, confronted his past, and embraced his future. The trials had tested him, but they had also shown him the strength and resilience he possessed.

As he left Eldridge Tower, the first light of dawn broke over the horizon. Eli knew that his journey was far from over, but he felt ready for whatever lay ahead. With the knowledge he had gained and the strength he had found, he was prepared to continue his quest for understanding and triumph.

10

The Veil of Truth

Eli stared at the towering edifice of the Celestial Archives, its ornate spires and gleaming façade almost mocking him with their grandeur. This was the final destination on his quest, a place said to hold the ultimate truth he sought. The Archives stood on a high hill, isolated from the rest of the world, as if guarding the secrets within with an almost palpable aura of mystery.

The evening sky was a deep indigo, and a light mist clung to the ground, adding an ethereal quality to the scene. Eli felt a shiver of anticipation and trepidation. The map had led him here, to this place where reality and illusion converged. He knew that within these walls, he would uncover the final piece of his grandfather's legacy—and, perhaps, his own destiny.

He approached the grand entrance, flanked by towering columns and inscribed with celestial symbols. The massive bronze doors stood slightly ajar, as if welcoming him in. As he pushed them open, the sound of creaking hinges echoed through the stillness, and a cool draft brushed against his face.

Inside, the Celestial Archives was an expansive, labyrinthine library filled with towering shelves of ancient tomes and manuscripts. The dim lighting from ornate chandeliers cast long shadows, creating an atmosphere of reverent silence. The only sound was the soft rustling of pages and the distant, rhythmic ticking of a grand clock somewhere in the depths of the building.

Eli walked cautiously between the aisles, his footsteps muffled by the thick carpet. The scent of aged paper and leather was strong, mingling with the faint aroma of incense that seemed to pervade the air. He knew he was searching for something specific—a hidden truth, a final revelation that would bring closure to his journey.

After what felt like hours of wandering, Eli came across a secluded alcove at the far end of the library. It was a circular room with a domed ceiling, and in the center stood a large, ancient pedestal. On the pedestal lay an intricately carved box, its surface covered in enigmatic symbols. Eli's heart quickened as he approached, the culmination of his quest seemingly within reach.

He reached for the box, but as his fingers brushed against it, the room seemed to shift. The walls and shelves began to blur and dissolve, leaving Eli in a disorienting void of swirling lights and shadows. He felt as if he was being pulled through a vortex, his sense of direction and time disintegrating.

When the sensation stopped, Eli found himself in a different place entirely. He stood in a grand hall, its walls adorned with celestial maps and star charts. The ceiling was a vast dome, its surface a mosaic of constellations and galaxies. At the center of the hall was a large, crystalline structure resembling a star—a source of blinding light that cast eerie, shifting patterns across the room.

The light seemed to beckon Eli, guiding him toward the crystalline structure. As he approached, the light intensified, and he heard a voice echoing through the hall—deep and resonant, yet strangely familiar.

"Eli, you have come far," the voice intoned. "But the truth you seek is not easily revealed. To uncover it, you must confront the veil that shrouds your reality."

Eli looked around, searching for the source of the voice. Shadows moved and shifted, forming into indistinct shapes that seemed to watch him with silent intensity. He felt a mixture of awe and anxiety as the voice continued.

"The veil of truth is not just a barrier but a reflection of your own fears and doubts. To see through it, you must first understand it. The truth lies not only in what is hidden but in what you are willing to confront."

Eli's mind raced. The trials he had faced had been physical, emotional, and psychological. This final challenge seemed to be an amalgamation of all he had endured. He knew he had to dig deeper, to confront the deepest parts of himself.

The light from the crystalline structure began to pulse, creating a rhythm that matched Eli's heartbeat. The patterns on the floor shifted, forming a labyrinth of light and shadow. Eli realized that the only way to move forward was to navigate this maze, to face whatever lay within it.

He stepped into the labyrinth, the light guiding his way. Each turn revealed new challenges—visions of his past failures, fears of the future, and doubts about his own worth. The labyrinth seemed to be a manifestation of his innermost struggles, a place where his greatest fears were brought to life.

Eli pressed on, his resolve unwavering. He remembered the lessons he had learned from his previous trials—the courage, the strength, and the clarity he had gained. He used these lessons to push through the illusions, to see beyond the veil.

As he reached the center of the labyrinth, the light intensified, and the walls dissolved, revealing a serene, open space bathed in a soft, golden glow. At the center of the space was a pedestal, and on it lay a single, open book. The pages were filled with a luminous script that seemed to pulse with a life of its own.

Eli approached the book, feeling a sense of reverence. As he read the pages, he saw the culmination of his journey—the ultimate truth. It was a revelation about the nature of reality, the interconnectedness of all things, and the power of understanding and embracing one's own path.

The book spoke of his grandfather's journey, his struggles, and his ultimate realization. It revealed that the true legacy was not just the knowledge he had sought but the wisdom he had gained through his trials. It was about understanding the self, confronting fears, and finding clarity in the midst of chaos.

As Eli finished reading, the light around him began to fade, and the Celestial Archives reappeared. The room was once again filled with the soft rustling of pages and the faint aroma of incense. The pedestal and the crystalline structure were gone, replaced by the familiar shelves and aisles of the library.

Eli felt a profound sense of peace and accomplishment. He had faced the final challenge, uncovered the ultimate truth, and completed his journey. The veil of truth had been lifted, revealing not just the knowledge he sought but a deeper understanding of himself.

As he left the Celestial Archives, the first light of dawn was breaking over the horizon. Eli felt ready to embrace whatever lay ahead, armed with the knowledge and wisdom he had gained. The journey had been long and arduous, but it had led him to a place of clarity and purpose. With the final piece of his grandfather's legacy revealed, he was prepared to continue his path and face whatever challenges the future held.

11

The Convergence of Shadows

Eli's mind buzzed with the revelations from the Celestial Archives as he approached the final destination of his journey: the enigmatic Obsidian Citadel. Perched on a rugged cliff overlooking a storm-swept sea, the Citadel's dark, angular towers seemed to pierce the turbulent sky. The wind howled through the rocky landscape, and the waves crashed violently against the cliffs, creating a constant roar that was both foreboding and hypnotic.

The Citadel was said to be a place where the boundaries between reality and the unknown were at their thinnest. It was a place of final convergence, where all paths intertwined and where the ultimate resolution of Eli's quest awaited him. As he climbed the steep path leading to the Citadel's entrance, he could feel the weight of anticipation and anxiety pressing down on him.

The path was treacherous, winding through jagged rocks and shrouded in dense mist. Eli had to move carefully, his flashlight cutting through the darkness as he navigated the slippery terrain. The storm seemed to intensify, with lightning flashing in the distance and thunder rumbling ominously. Each step seemed to echo the pounding of his heart.

Finally, he reached the towering gates of the Obsidian Citadel. The gates were massive, wrought iron adorned with intricate designs of mythical creatures and ancient symbols. They were slightly ajar, as if inviting him in. Eli hesitated for a moment, then pushed the gates open, their creaking hinges blending with the roar of the storm.

Inside, the Citadel was a labyrinth of shadowed corridors and echoing chambers. The air was cool and heavy, filled with the scent of damp stone and aged wood. Eli's flashlight revealed dimly lit hallways, their walls adorned with faded tapestries and ancient symbols that seemed to writhe and shift in the flickering light.

He followed a series of winding passages, each turn leading him deeper into the heart of the Citadel. The further he went, the more oppressive the atmosphere became. The corridors seemed to close in around him, their walls reflecting distorted images that played tricks on his senses. He felt a creeping unease, as if he were being watched by unseen eyes.

As he rounded a corner, Eli found himself in a grand hall, its vaulted ceiling supported by towering columns. The hall was filled with the low hum of an unseen force, and the floor was covered in a mosaic of dark, interlocking patterns. In the center of the hall stood a large, circular altar, surrounded by flickering candles and strange artifacts.

Approaching the altar, Eli saw that it was covered with a variety of ancient objects—arcane symbols, shards of crystal, and weathered scrolls. At the center of the altar lay a large, obsidian orb, its surface reflecting a swirling vortex of shadows. The orb seemed to pulse with a dark energy, drawing Eli's gaze irresistibly.

He reached out to touch the orb, but as his fingers brushed against its surface, the room was plunged into darkness. The sudden shift was disorienting, and Eli could hear the distant sound of whispers and murmurs, growing louder and more insistent. He fumbled for his flashlight, but the beam did little to penetrate the suffocating darkness.

The whispers coalesced into a single, echoing voice that seemed to come from all directions. "Eli, you have come to the heart of the Citadel. The final test awaits you, a confrontation with the shadows that lie within."

The darkness began to shift and swirl, forming into indistinct shapes and figures. Eli saw fleeting glimpses of faces and forms, each one a distorted reflection of his own fears and doubts. The shadows seemed to be alive, moving with an unsettling intelligence, as if they were manifestations of his own inner turmoil.

Eli steeled himself, recalling the lessons he had learned throughout his journey. He had faced his past, confronted his fears, and uncovered profound truths. Now, he needed to face the ultimate manifestation of his fears—the shadows of his own psyche.

The shadows began to take on more concrete forms, becoming monstrous and threatening. They advanced toward Eli, their movements slow and deliberate. Eli felt a surge of fear, but he forced himself to focus, drawing on the strength he had gained from his previous trials.

He remembered the power of light and clarity, the lessons from the Celestial Archives. With a deep breath, he activated the orb, holding it high above his head. The orb's dark energy began to resonate with his own inner light, creating a counterforce against the shadows.

As the shadows writhed and recoiled, Eli felt a sense of empowerment. The darkness was no longer an insurmountable force but a reflection of his own struggles. He faced it head-on, using the light of the orb to push back against the encroaching darkness.

The battle was intense and exhausting, but Eli's resolve remained unshaken.

He knew that the shadows were a part of him, and by confronting them, he was not only facing his fears but also reclaiming his own strength and clarity. The orb's light grew brighter, forcing the shadows to retreat and dissolve.

As the darkness lifted, the grand hall of the Citadel reappeared. The oppressive atmosphere had lifted, replaced by a sense of calm and resolution. The obsidian orb had transformed into a simple, radiant crystal, its surface reflecting a soft, warm light.

Eli felt a profound sense of achievement. He had faced the ultimate test and emerged victorious. The shadows of his fears had been vanquished, and he had gained a deeper understanding of himself.

As he left the Obsidian Citadel, the storm outside had subsided, and the first rays of dawn began to break through the clouds. Eli felt a renewed sense of purpose and clarity. The journey had been long and arduous, but it had led him to a place of profound insight and resolution.

With the final piece of his grandfather's legacy revealed and his own inner demons confronted, Eli was ready to embrace the future. The path ahead was uncertain, but he felt prepared to face whatever challenges lay ahead, armed with the strength and wisdom he had gained from his journey.

12

The Threshold of Eternity

Eli's journey had led him through trials of fire and shadow, through mazes of light and darkness, and now he stood at the edge of the most formidable challenge of all: the Threshold of Eternity. The location, known only from cryptic references in ancient texts, was a mythical place said to exist beyond the bounds of time and reality. It was where the final truths were revealed, where the essence of existence itself was laid bare.

The path to the Threshold was marked by a solitary stone archway perched high on a windswept plateau. The archway seemed to shimmer in the twilight, its edges blurred as if the fabric of reality was being stretched and distorted. The air was filled with an eerie silence, and the sky above was an unsettling blend of colors, swirling and shifting like an unspoken riddle.

Eli approached the archway, feeling a deep sense of foreboding. Each step seemed to echo with the weight of his experiences, each breath carried the burden of the revelations he had yet to encounter. He reached the archway and looked through it, but what lay beyond was not visible—just an endless expanse of shifting, nebulous light and shadow.

Taking a deep breath, he stepped through the archway. The sensation was immediate and disorienting, as though he was being pulled through a vortex of shimmering energy. His surroundings twisted and warped, and the familiar world fell away, replaced by a vast, otherworldly expanse.

When the sensation subsided, Eli found himself in a place unlike any he had ever seen. The ground beneath him was a swirling mist of glowing colors, and the sky above was a shifting tapestry of stars and constellations, ever-changing and dynamic. The horizon seemed to stretch infinitely in all directions, and the air was filled with a faint, harmonious hum.

In the center of this surreal realm was a massive, translucent sphere, suspended in mid-air. It pulsed with a soft, radiant light, and Eli could see swirling patterns and images within it—visions of past events, future possibilities, and the intricate web of existence itself.

As he approached the sphere, a figure materialized beside it—a being of pure light and energy, its form shifting and flowing like a living aurora. The figure's presence was both overwhelming and comforting, radiating a profound sense of wisdom and serenity.

"Welcome, Eli," the figure intoned, its voice resonating with a deep, melodic harmony. "You stand at the Threshold of Eternity, a place where the boundaries of time and reality converge. Here, you will come face-to-face with the ultimate truth."

Eli felt a mixture of awe and apprehension. "What is the ultimate truth?"

The figure's form shimmered as it replied. "The truth you seek is not just about knowledge or understanding. It is about the essence of existence, the interconnectedness of all things, and the profound realization that every moment, every choice, shapes the tapestry of reality."

With a wave of its hand, the figure directed Eli's attention to the sphere. The images within it began to coalesce, forming a series of interconnected scenes— moments of joy, sorrow, triumph, and despair. Eli saw the lives of countless individuals, their experiences intertwining in a complex, beautiful pattern.

The figure continued, "This sphere represents the cosmic web of existence, a tapestry woven from the threads of every life, every choice, every action. It is a reflection of the interconnectedness of all things, the unity of all experiences."

As Eli gazed at the sphere, he saw his own life's moments interwoven with those of others. He saw how his actions had ripple effects, how his choices had influenced the lives around him, and how the lessons he had learned had contributed to the greater whole.

A profound realization washed over him. The ultimate truth was not a singular answer or revelation but an understanding of the interconnectedness of all things, the way every action and choice contributed to the grand tapestry of existence.

The figure's voice grew softer, more contemplative. "The Threshold of Eternity is not a place of finality but of transformation. By understanding the unity of all things, you gain insight into the nature of reality and your place within it."

Eli felt a deep sense of peace and clarity. The trials he had faced, the challenges he had overcome, had all been leading to this moment of profound realization. He understood that his journey was not just about seeking answers but about embracing the interconnectedness of all things, recognizing the impact of his choices and actions.

The sphere's light grew brighter, enveloping Eli in a warm, radiant glow. He felt himself becoming one with the cosmic web, his own essence merging with the greater whole. The boundaries of self and other, of time and space, dissolved, leaving him with a profound sense of unity and purpose.

As the light receded, Eli found himself back at the edge of the stone archway, the surreal realm of the Threshold of Eternity fading behind him. The sky above was once again a familiar twilight, and the ground beneath him was solid and real. The archway stood silent and still, a gateway between worlds.

Eli took a deep breath, feeling a renewed sense of clarity and purpose. He had faced the ultimate challenge, uncovered the profound truth of interconnectedness, and emerged with a greater understanding of himself and the world around him.

With the final piece of his journey complete, Eli felt ready to embrace the future with a sense of peace and empowerment. The lessons he had learned, the truths he had uncovered, would guide him as he continued his path, armed with the knowledge that every moment, every choice, was a part of the grand tapestry of existence.

As he walked away from the Threshold of Eternity, the horizon beckoned with new possibilities, and Eli felt a deep sense of fulfillment. The journey had been long and arduous, but it had led him to a place of profound insight and understanding. With the ultimate truth revealed, he was prepared to face whatever challenges lay ahead, confident in the knowledge that he was a vital thread in the intricate fabric of reality.